Dear Parent:
Your child's love of reading starts here!

Every child learns to read in a different way and at his or her own speed. Some go back and forth between reading levels and read favorite books again and again. Others read through each level in order. You can help your young reader improve and become more confident by encouraging his or her own interests and abilities. From books your child reads with you to the first books he or she reads alone, there are I Can Read Books for every stage of reading:

SHARED READING
Basic language, word repetition, and whimsical illustrations, ideal for sharing with your emergent reader

BEGINNING READING
Short sentences, familiar words, and simple concepts for children eager to read on their own

READING WITH HELP
Engaging stories, longer sentences, and language play for developing readers

READING ALONE
Complex plots, challenging vocabulary, and high-interest topics for the independent reader

ADVANCED READING
Short paragraphs, chapters, and exciting themes for the perfect bridge to chapter books

I Can Read Books have introduced children to the joy of reading since 1957. Featuring award-winning authors and illustrators and a fabulous cast of beloved characters, I Can Read Books set the standard for beginning readers.

A lifetime of discovery begins with the magical words "I Can Read!"

Visit www.icanread.com for information
on enriching your child's reading experience.

*I'm Rappy the Raptor
and I'd like to say,
I may not talk
in the usual way.*

RAPPY

Goes to the Supermarket

To Tamar —D.G.

To Nick —T.B.

I Can Read Book® is a trademark of HarperCollins Publishers.

Rappy Goes to the Supermarket
Text copyright © 2017 by Dan Gutman
Illustrations copyright © 2017 by Tim Bowers
All rights reserved. Manufactured in China.
No part of this book may be used or reproduced in any manner whatsoever without written permission except in the case
of brief quotations embodied in critical articles and reviews. For information address HarperCollins Children's Books, a
division of HarperCollins Publishers, 195 Broadway, New York, NY 10007.
www.icanread.com

ISBN 978-0-06-225262-3 (pbk.)
ISBN 978-0-06-225263-0 (hardcover)

16 17 18 19 20 SCP 10 9 8 7 6 5 4 3 2 1   ❖   First Edition

ead!™

READING
2
WITH HELP

RAPPY
Goes to the Supermarket

by Dan Gutman

illustrated by Tim Bowers

HARPER
An Imprint of HarperCollinsPublishers

I'm rappin' and snappin'
all the time.
Whenever I talk,
I'm talkin' in rhyme.

I'm rapping in the basement.

I'm rapping in the kitchen.

I rap when a mosquito bites
and really gets me itchin'.

My mom said, "Let's go!

I have errands to run."

I'd rather stay home.

Errands aren't any fun.

"Rappy!" Mom hollered.

"We've got to go out."

I rolled my eyes and began to pout.

"Where are you taking me?

I really want to know.

Why are you making me?

I don't want to go!"

"Are we going to the cleaners?

Are we going on vacation?

Are we going to the car wash?

Or maybe the gas station?"

Mom pulled the car into a lot.

She couldn't find a parking spot.

Then at last she finally parked it . . .

. . . We were at the supermarket!

Buying stuff is such a drag.

Mom got out her shopping bags.

Supermarkets are so boring.

I already feel like snoring.

"Wait a minute," Mommy said.

"There's something that I missed.

How can I do my shopping?

I forgot my shopping list!"

"Don't worry, Mom," I said.

"We don't need to go home.

I remember all that stuff.

I wrote a little poem!"

"Mustard! Custard!

Cornflakes! Cupcakes!

Pork chops! Cough drops!

Cold cuts! Peanuts!

Apple fritter! Kitty litter!

Clam chowder! Foot powder!

Chips and dips and bacon strips!"

Mom and I went down each aisle.

I think we must have walked a mile.

They have a million kinds of cheese,

breads, and honey made by bees.

Cookies, gum, and juice in jars.

Look at all those candy bars!

Treats and goodies make me drool.

Hey, supermarkets can be cool!

We got a dozen jumbo eggs.

Some milk, some cake, and turkey legs.

Toothpaste and a windshield scraper.

But what about . . . "THE TOILET
PAPER?!"

"Oh, never mind," Mom said.

"Forget it."

"No, Mom," I said.

"I'll go get it!"

I told Mom I'd do my best.

And I set out on my quest.

I'd search the shelves

to reach my goal

and find the toilet paper rolls.

Supermarkets are amazin'!

They have seven kinds of raisins!

Pretzels and crackers for hungry snackers.

They could feed the Green Bay Packers!

Oodles of noodles and all kinds of goop.

They have soup that helps you poop!

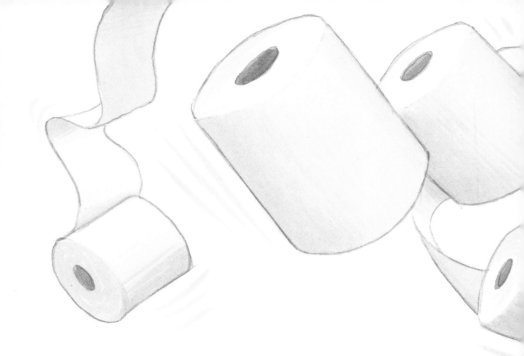

At last I found what I was needing.

In my chest my heart was beating.

But when I pulled one roll from under,

there came a sound a lot like thunder.

I knew that it was time to go

when someone yelled, "Watch out below!"

And then that toilet paper mountain

rained down upon me like a fountain!

"Help!" I shouted.

Then I said,

"There's toilet paper

on my head!"

The manager came running over.

His name tag said to call him Grover.

He didn't look like he was happy

when I said my name was Rappy.

The manager said, "You're a pest.

You made a mess.

And now I'm feeling lots of stress.

I'm gonna scream and lose control,

Unless you pick up every roll!"

27

I was feeling kind of sick.

I had to think of something quick.

"Attention, shoppers! In aisle four,

there is something on the floor.

Something that I know you need.

This stuff works. It's guaranteed!

It never fails. It won't get stale.

And today only, it's on sale!

You can wear it on your head,

or give it to your uncle Fred.

You could get some for your cousin.

I think you should buy a dozen!

But just in case you forgot 'em,

This is something for your bottom!"

"I'll take three," some lady said.

"I can store them in my shed."

"I want ten," yelled one tall man,

who put them in his minivan.

"Give me some," said another.

"I can share them with my brother."

In the end, the floor was clean
and Grover was no longer mean.

He didn't scream and he didn't yell.

He just said, "This kid can sell!"

I'm Rappy the Raptor

and I'd like to say,

I may not talk in the usual way.

I love hopping and I love bopping.

And now I know that I love shopping!